CW00327435

Finches

A guide to selection, care, housing, nutrition, behaviour, health, breeding and species

the Content

Common Grenadier

Foreword

Keeping birds is a wonderful hobby which has thousands of fans in the UK. Birds draw our attention by their ability to fly, their colours, their beautiful songs and their exuberant behaviour. It is quite easy to understand why birds attract so many people.

This book is specifically aimed at bird enthusiasts who keep finches in an aviary or an indoor cage, or those who are considering doing so. An experienced enthusiast will also find many useful tips here. All aspects of keeping finches are covered here, including caging, buying, advantages and disadvantages of the different species, care, health and breeding. We have also included a list of useful contacts. The species described in this book include some that are most commonly kept and that are also suitable for beginners, but also a number of bird families that need a bit more attention. To make it short, we have included anything a beginning bird enthusiast needs to know. This book also gives an up-to-date insight into the bird lovers' world with all its different aspects, and we also pay attention to the organized bird breeding sport.

The authors Jan de Nijs and Piet Onderdelinden have both been aviculturists since youth and have years of experience in keeping and breeding different bird species. Both are judges with the 'Nederlandse Bond voor Vogelliefhebbers' (NBvV, Dutch Association of Bird Enthusiasts). They work together in the field of bird photography and write articles for various national and international bird magazines and bird books. They are active in a number of functions in organized bird keeping. Jan is chairman of the 'Nederlandse Zebravinken Club' (NZC, Dutch Zebra Finches Club), TC-member of European songbirds and lecturer in the training of judges. Piet is chairman of the 'Parkieten Speciaal Club' (PSC, Special Parakeet Club), where he is also chairman of the technical commission for large parakeets.

About Pets

A Publication of About Pets.

About Pets
co-publisher United Kingdom
Kingdom Books
PO9 5TL, England

ISBN 1852792043
First printing
April 2005

Original title: *de Praktische Vinkenwijzer*
© 2005 Welzo Media Productions bv,
Warffum, the Netherlands
http://www.overdieren.nl

Photos:
Piet Onderdelinden, Jan de Nijs and
Rob Dekker

Printed in China through Printworks Int. Ltd.

Buying your first birds

If you are thinking about buying one or more birds, it is good to be clear about the consequences in advance.

Chestnut-breasted Munia

You are taking on the responsibility for a living creature for some time to come. It is definitely not our intention to talk you out of this idea, as you can have a lot of fun keeping birds. You need to understand what it involves before you get started, however. Keeping a pet means that you need to make sure that your pet gets everything it needs. It cannot go looking for food itself, as it depends on you for this. Do you have anyone to look after your pet when you go on holiday, for example?

If you decide to go ahead and buy some birds, there are several ways you can proceed. The first one is to go to a shop or dealer. Here you can find both finches that breeders have given away as excess, as well as several imported species. In the bird scene, almost all birds are ringed with a solid ring. The second possibility is to buy your birds at a bird fair. These are held all over the UK and you can find them announced in bird magazines and on the Internet. At fairs you will encounter dealers, but also enthusiasts who offer their birds for sale. For those of you who are seriously considering breeding birds, the third option is probably the best: to visit some bird breeders. Here you can choose one or more birds. You will also get the chance to see how the birds are caged and what they are fed. Serious breeders also frequently enter competitions and the quality of their birds is therefore often better. The best breeders end up high in the rankings at shows. Bird shows are held all over the country, especially in the autumn. Nowadays, the Internet also gives you a chance to search for breeders' sites. Some breeders offer their birds for sale there and you may find whole price lists.

What to watch out for

Wherever you may buy finches, make sure that they are as healthy as possible. You cannot look inside a bird, but you can often determine whether something is wrong by its appearance. Never buy a bird that is sitting in its cage with watering eyes and raised feathers. It is obviously not well. A healthy bird is lively, holds its feathers against its body, especially when you approach the cage, and is shiny.

Any bird you might consider buying also has to be clean. It must not have any dirty plumage at the anus, as this can be a sign of intestinal problems. It is not a big problem if the bird is missing a nail, but if it is missing whole toes, then it will not be able to hold onto the perch during mating and might thus produce unfertilised eggs. So avoid buying such birds. It is also not a big problem if the bird is missing a few feathers or if some have broken off, but it has to be able to fly well, so the wings must be intact.

When buying your birds, also pay attention to their cage or aviary. A dirty, musty environment harbours a lot of health risks (bacteria, etc.).

Age

It is important that you know the age of any birds you want to buy, especially if you are buying birds for the first time and have little experience. It is best to buy young birds which have not been used for breeding yet. In pet shops you often find older birds. You don't know their background and there is no way you can find out. These might be birds that don't breed or only badly. Be aware of the fact that finches can often only reproduce until they are three to five years old.

You can sometimes buy good breeding pairs from reliable addresses. If you are looking for birds with which you can start breeding straight away, choose birds which are approximately a year old. If the bird is ringed, you can determine the age from the number of the year of issue, which you can find next to the number for the breeder, the number of the issuing organisation and the serial number.

Difference cock and hen

In most species, the male is more vividly coloured than the female. This is called sexual dimorphism.

Gouldian Finches

Himalayan Greenfinch

Yellow-crowned Bishop

If there is no visible sexual difference between birds, they are often put apart. After a week a hen is placed with them. If the unknown bird is a male, it will start singing immediately. Put a coloured flexible ring on those cocks and you will be able to identify them from a distance.

In the case of imported birds with no visible difference between sexes, it is advisable to buy several pairs. Put a coloured flexible ring on each bird and leave them together. See which birds pair up and note it according to the coloured rings. You can then put pairs together this way.

In some species the hen even has a completely different colour.

There are some species where there is no visual difference between sexes, such as canaries. Here you can only determine the sex by blowing the plumage around the anus to the side. On hens, you will see an oval genital, whereas the cock has obvious genitalia. This is called a 'tap' in bird terms. The difference is not yet as visible in younger birds, but it is easy to spot in the breeding season. Another difference between cock and hen is the song. Male birds sing, whereas female birds might utter the odd tone, but this is nowhere near the male's song.

Nowadays it is also possible to determine birds' sexes with the help of a DNA test. You will have to make sure that you will be able to identify the birds with the help of a solid ring or a flexible ring.

Buying standard birds
Buying breeding birds with the aim to enter shows with the young is a different story. It is advisable to become a member of a bird association or one of the specialist clubs mentioned later in the book. Here you will find experts who can guide you in their respective avucultural field. They will also be able to advise you when you buy your breeding pairs.

There are different standards for many bird species. The standard describes which requirements a bird must fulfil to enter bird shows. If you intend to participate in bird shows, you should acquaint yourself with the demands placed on the birds. Also inform yourself about the rules and customs practised within the respective association and at shows. Visit information evenings and try to get to know some experienced breeders who could help you.

Here's a good piece of advice for beginning bird breeders: do not spend too much money when buying your first birds. Start with some simple but healthy finches and try to breed some young to gain experience. If you are sure that the species you have chosen is the right one for you, you can try to buy some better birds at a good breeder's, for example. Be aware that top birds are often only for sale for top money. This is a question of supply and demand, as everyone wants to buy their birds from a champion.

Aviculturists often speak about breeding lines. A number of top breeders have established their own lines over time, and they are all known for some particular characteristics. Lines can stand out through the length of the bird, the type, the intensity of the colour, markings or good

breeding results. These characteristics are also best preserved in such lines. If you start crossing with birds from a totally different line, this might end in bad breeding results. This is a known fact among bird enthusiasts. To avoid disappointments, it is advisable to purchase birds from one breeder only. This will give you more certainty in predicting that the descendants of these birds will also be good.

Experienced breeders do combine birds from different lines when they want to improve certain characteristics in their birds. To start with crossing birds from different lines, you need experience and 'feeling', which you will hardly get from a book. Experienced breeders know which bloodlines they can combine with each other, because they know their origins. The best way to gain the necessary experience is to talk to breeders at specialist clubs and by visiting a lot of shows where you should look at and compare the finches. Obtain plenty of information from experienced breeders at the beginning and ask if one of them will advise you in purchasing your birds.

Double-barred Finch

Plum-headed Finch

Feeding your finches

Most finch species live primarily on plant food and especially on (grass) seeds. During the breeding season they gather as many fresh and unripe seeds as possible for their young.

These contain a lot of vitamins and nutrients which are important for the young birds. They are also more easily digestible than the hard dry seeds. In the breeding season, some finch species add insects and/or larvae to their menu. There are also species that only eat insects or fruit.

Feeding in the aviary

Most enthusiasts, no matter whether they keep their birds as pets or for breeding, feed them ready-made (commercial) seed mixes. These mixes contain different sorts of seeds and there are different mixes for different species, e.g. Australian Finch food. The complete mixes are sold in pet shops in different sizes. The bigger the package, the more economical it is. If you

only keep one bird at home a 1 kg package will last you several weeks. Breeders with dozens of breeding pairs will buy their food in bulk loads of 25 kg. Some breeders mix their own feeds and buy the different seeds separately. It is not worth the effort for just a pet bird or a couple of breeding pairs, and a ready-made seed mix from the shop will be sufficient.

Besides seed mix, your birds will need some more things to stay healthy, such as:

Egg food

All pet shops sell different brands of egg food. It is a necessary complementary food to the seed mixes, because it contains a number of important vitamins and minerals. During the breeding season your birds should be fed egg food every day. The young can digest this much more easily than hard seeds. During the moulting season your birds also need these nutrients every day to be able to renew their plumage.

In the rest period, which is the time between the moulting and the breeding period, it is sufficient to feed your birds egg food two or three times a week. You should increase the number of times you feed egg food towards the breeding season in order to get your birds into good breeding condition. Laying eggs and raising young demands a lot from your birds.

Green food and fruit

You can try around to find out what your birds like best. Some birds like to eat something green, such as lettuce, endives, a piece of apple, some carrot, etc. Make sure that you wash everything properly. Never give your birds too much at once, but only feed them small portions which they can eat in a short time. Green food contains a lot of water and not very many nutrients. It is more useful for keeping your birds occupied and to give them something other than seeds once in a while. Too much food with a high water content can lead to intestinal problems. Therefore remove any green food that

hasn't been eaten from the cage soon, as it goes off quickly (mould can develop).

Grass and weed seeds

You can also try to entice your birds with grass and weed seeds. You can always just pick grass and weeds from your garden, your birds will certainly like them. You will also find chickweed in almost any garden: a small green plant with very small white flowers. The stalks contain a white milky fluid. You can hang up a large bundle of grass and weed seeds in your aviary, and you will find that your birds will enjoy them and be occupied for quite a while. Be very careful where you pick weeds and grass. Never pick them next to a busy road because of exhaust fumes, and also not from ground that has recently been treated with pesticides.

Egg food

Seeds

Millet

Sepia

Pin-tailed Whydah

Millet

The millet that you can buy on stems is a little softer than that in seed mixes. It is therefore ideal to help young birds learn to eat by themselves. The birds also have a lot of fun eating millet from the stems.

Supplements

Besides the above feeds, your birds also need a number of supplements:

Calcium

Grit (finely ground shells) ensures that the birds get enough calcium. They have to be offered this every day. You can buy grit separately, but it is usually contained in the shell sand you use as a floor covering. Another way of providing calcium is to offer your birds the carapace of the squid (sepia). You can buy sepia in any pet shop. You can also grind eggshells and feed them to your birds. It is advisable to heat these (boil them in water) to kill off any bacteria or germs.

Stomach gravel

These are very fine stones that the birds ingest. They stay within the gizzard and help to grind down the seeds.

Iodine blocks

These blocks contain a lot of minerals, such as iodine which prevents problems of the thyroid gland. The blocks also give your birds a good opportunity to gnaw, which keeps the beak in good shape.

Vitamins and minerals

Whole books have been written about these. They are vital for any living creature and ailments develop if there is a lack of vitamins and minerals. Overdosing can also cause problems, however. It will not do any harm to give your birds a course of vitamins at the beginning of the breeding season. Make sure you feed them a product which is adjusted to the needs of birds and which contains all the vitamins and minerals in the right proportions. Your birds will normally receive all the vitamins and minerals they need from a balanced diet and giving them extra vitamins is not normally necessary. A sufficient and well balanced diet is better than a medical closet with all sorts of vitamins and solutions.

Water

Every living being consists of water to a large percentage. It is

therefore essential that your birds have access to clean drinking water every day. It depends on the species how much water it needs. Birds originating from the rain forest will drink more than birds from savannah areas. The latter almost always have a split tongue, which allows them to suck up drops of morning dew. Other species have a flat tongue and need to drink more.

However much a bird drinks per day, it is still necessary to rinse the water bottle and fill it with clean water every day. Drinking water becomes soiled very quickly, and mould and bacteria grow particularly quickly in warm weather. They can make your bird seriously ill. Under the influence of light, algae might also grow in the water bottle. The transparent part of the bottle will slowly turn green or brown. Algae are slimy and they allow bacteria to develop. You can buy darker coloured drinking bottles in pet shops, in which algae do not grow as quickly.

You can easily clean drinking bottles with a bottlebrush or by putting them in a chlorine solution for a few hours. Make sure that you rinse them well afterwards.

Daily care

To summarise it briefly, daily care consists of refreshing the drinking water and feeding seeds and/or egg food. Take into consideration that drinking bottles can also leak once in a while.

You need to check the seed container every day. It sometimes appears to be still full, whereas it is actually only covered in husks. The birds peel the seeds and leave the empty husks behind. You can blow the empty husks out of the container and then you will see how many seeds remain. If you are going on holiday you need to make your bird sitter aware of this. It would not be the first time that birds starved to death while it looked as if their feed bowl was still full. I think that every pet shop has clients in during the holiday period who are looking for a bird that looks exactly like the poor thing that starved to death in the short time that they were supposed to look after it.

Remove any uneaten egg food and possibly green food from the cage every day to prevent bacteria growth.

Drinking bottle

Caging

Most bird species can be kept in the living room without too many problems. There are many different types of cages, which you can buy in pet shops. With some DIY skills you can also make a suitable cage yourself.

Layard black-headed weaver

In the living room

If you don't want to find feathers, sand and empty husks on the floor, then you should keep your birds outdoors. Birds are messy. This is unavoidable, but you can collect the mess under or in front of the cage so that it is not spread throughout the house. Birds also excrete a certain substance through their feathers, which some people are allergic to.

The size of the cage or indoor aviary depends on the number of birds you want to keep. Make sure that the birds have enough space for flying. A narrow high cage is less suitable than a longer one, as birds usually fly horizontally and hardly ever vertically. Also, don't clutter the cage with too many toys which would decrease the flying space.

A cage should be at least 50 cm long for one or two birds the size of canaries.

Where to put the cage

Place the cage for your birds on a well-lit place in your living room. Never put it in front of a window where the birds would be exposed to sunlight all day. Birds do enjoy sitting in the sun, but they must be able to decide when they'd rather be in the shade. The best place for a cage is against a wall. Birds also feel safer here, as people can only walk around the cage on one side. If the cage is standing or hanging in a position where people can walk around it on different sides, the birds cannot withdraw and feel less secure.

Make sure that your birds are not standing in a draught, as they cannot cope with this. Make sure

Finches

that the cage is placed steadily on a table, a stand or a console. A cage that hangs from a chain and moves every time the birds do makes its inhabitants feel very insecure. This will make them very shy.

Fitting out a cage

The interior of a finch cage can be quite simple. Make sure that they have plenty of perches which are attached safely. Too many perches decrease the flying space, however. The perches must be thick enough that the birds can clasp them well. It is best to use perches of varying thickness, as these are best for the birds' muscles. Some cages have thin plastic perches delivered as standard. For a few pence you can replace these with wooden perches of 12 to 15 mm thickness from the DIY store. Willow twigs also make good perches.

It is best to cover the floor of a cage with aviary sand. This usually contains grit which the

birds can ingest. At present, you can buy a number of different floor coverings which all have their own advantages and disadvantages. Let the shop assistant advise you on this. Some people will advise you to use old newspapers as floor covering because it can hold a lot of fluid and is easy to replace. A disadvantage of newspapers is, however, the ink which is harmful to animals and humans alike. If you do use newspapers on the floor, then make sure that you offer your birds grit and stomach gravel in a separate bowl.

Make sure that your birds can easily reach their food and drink bowls or bottles. A bird might have some problems finding its food when it comes into a new cage. So scatter some food on the floor, this will help the bird get used to its new cage.

For a pet bird, some toys can offer distraction in its cage. You can choose from a large variety of

mirrors, bells, ladders etc, in pet shops. Remember, however, not to clutter the cage with toys. Tropical birds have fairly little use for toys, it is better to buy them a companion.

Outdoor aviary

If you have enough space in your garden you can build an outdoor aviary. Take any limitations into account. Building regulations vary per community. Find out before starting your aviary whether you need a permit. Also ask your neighbours whether they would mind.

A suitable aviary consists of a flight with a night shelter attached to it. A lot of bird breeders have a breeding room indoors and one or more outdoor flights where those birds that are not used for breeding can fly. Some bids breed in colonies in the wild, whereas some only brood as pairs. Bigger species often require an aviary to themselves, but smaller species can often be placed in a so-called communal aviary. It is also important to know something about their natural behaviour and the background of the birds.

The size and position of the aviary is, of course, determined by the space available. If you can choose, then an aviary facing east or west is ideal. It is inadvisable to let an aviary face south, as it is then standing in the full sun. North is also not a good option, as it gets dark too quickly and is very cold in the winter. You need to make sure that the aviary is protected against the full sun in the summer and the wind and rain in the colder seasons. Most outdoor aviaries for birds have a roof, even if it is transparent. This keeps the aviary dry and prevents the floor and the perches from being soiled with the faeces of wild birds (which can transfer diseases). It also offers some protection against birds of prey and cats etc.

Building materials

You can use a number of materials to build an aviary. Today the frames of outdoor

aviaries are often made of square aluminium tubes. You can buy different couplings for them, which means that building an aviary is quite easy for someone with some basic DIY skills. The material is quite expensive but it needs very little maintenance. Wood is a cheaper alternative, but it is less durable.

You can buy the mesh per meter from a roll in larger bird specialist shops or at the ironmonger's. The mesh does not need to be too heavy for finches. The mesh has usually been galvanised to prevent rusting. New mesh usually shines quite a lot, which can be a nuisance. You can cover it with a darker paint that isn't harmful to birds. This allows a better view of the birds but it also keeps the mesh in good condition longer.

Floor
The floor of the outdoor flight must be dry. A wet floor is a breeding ground for bacteria. Plants in the aviary are not advisable for all finches, as canaries, for example, will destroy them within no time. An aviary with plants attracts insects, which is an extra source of food for many species, but it is generally too little to raise young with it in the breeding season. You need to offer the birds some extra live food then. The interior of an outdoor aviary can vary. The more plants you put in your

aviary the less you will be able to see your birds. They will hide away and stay very shy.

Perches
You can make perches from turned wood which you can buy in varying lengths in the DIY shop. Many enthusiasts build rows of perches neatly placed one under the other. You can also use twigs from trees. A twisted twig or ragged tree trunk is not only decorative but also gives your birds something to do. There need to be plenty of sitting opportunities in the aviary, but flying space is just as important. Take into considerations that birds like to sleep as high up as possible. If there is little space high up, this can lead to fights.

Night shelter
Because of the danger of nightly disturbances in the aviary through birds of prey and cats, it is best if you get your birds used to spending the night in their shelter. The night shelter should therefore be a little higher than the flight. It needs to have highly placed perches and a window so that it stays light as long as possible in the evenings. The finches will then look for a safe sleeping place indoors. If this is not working you can lock the birds up in the shelter at night. The space and number of perches inside determines on the number of birds that you can keep in the aviary.

Diamond Firetail

Ultramarine
Grosbeak

as a flight for young birds. Young birds are independent at approximately six weeks and most pairs will then go over to laying their next batch. It happens quite often that the older birds then see the young as rivals and chase after them in an attempt to chase them away. This can even end in the death of some of the youngsters. You can prevent this by taking them out of the aviary in time. After the breeding season they can quite happily be placed together again.

The feed and drink containers are best attached to the inside. You can place them on the ground, but it is better if they are a little higher. The bowls are then not soiled as easily by the birds and they are also more difficult to reach for vermin, such as mice. If you release new birds into the aviary, do that in the night shelter, so that they can find the food straight away. Introduce new birds as early in the day as possible and not shortly before it gets dark. They then have plenty of time to get used to their new home and to find the food and drink.

The night shelter needs to provide access to the aviary by one or more hatches. Make sure that you can open and close these from outside, so that you don't have to enter the aviary every time you want to open or close them. Cover the windows with mesh so that the birds don't fly against them. This mesh also prevents your finches escaping if a window should get broken for some reason. You can also integrate a door between night shelter and flight. A door directly at the flight also has the risk that your birds escape unless you build a sluice around it.

If you want to breed with your birds, then it is advisable to create an extra room in the night shelter

As you can see we can only provide some general advice on building aviaries here. It is useless to show you all sorts of plans and designs as your personal circumstances determine what your aviary will look like. It is best to go and visit some breeders, as they will usually be able to give you the best advice on building aviaries.

The inhabitants

Canaries cohabitate quite easily, even to the degree that a few males can live together with more hens. European songbirds are best kept in pairs. You can put several species together but make sure that there is always only one pair per species. European songbirds can also be kept together with canaries. Tropical bird species can be kept outdoors as long as you put them in the aviary in the summer so that they have plenty of time to get used to the outdoors before it turns winter. A solid night shelter is then very advisable. This also applies to other finch species, such as Zebra Finches, Society Finches, Java Sparrows, Shafttails, Indian Silverbills and African Silverbills. The small African finches, such as the Red-cheeked Cordonbleu, the Red-billed Fire Finch etc. can also be kept outdoors without too many problems. Pet shops with a larger assortment sell heated perches, which the birds use very happily when it is freezing, as their feet are very sensitive to frost.

Breeding room

If you decided to breed birds for competition or if you want to breed certain colour combinations, you need to have

cages in which you can place the separate pairs, as you need to be able to pair the birds up as you want to. You will have to pay attention to colour, size, relationship, etc. If you let the birds choose their partners in the aviary you might end up with less desirable combinations, which is why you need breeding cages. A lot of breeders use a spare room or a shed to establish a breeding room. This consists of a number of breeding cages and one or more flights placed against one wall. When furnishing the room you obviously need to take windows and doors into consideration.

Breeding cages

If you are any good at DIY you can quite easily make breeding cages yourself. You can buy

Gloster Canaries

yourself from metal or mesh. Most enthusiasts use ready-made front panels as you can buy them in pet shops in different sizes and styles. They have a door and maybe some flaps for plastic food containers. You can also simply put feeding bowls on the floor. The front panels are very suitable for hanging up water dispensers.

If you intend to build your own cages it is best to buy the front panels first and only start to assemble the cages when you have all the right measurements. You can cover the rough edges of the panels with an aluminium or plastic strip, which you can normally buy in the most common widths.

If you are no good at DIY, then you can choose from a number of ready-made cages. Different vendors normally have their stands at big shows and fairs, and you can also find different contact details in the classified sections of bird magazines. The cages will not be cheap but it is an investment in something you will use for years to come. They are assembled without screws or nails and you can sometimes take them apart yourself. These system cages often have removable partitions. If you remove these partitions you can offer your birds big flying' cages. You might be lucky enough to get some second-hand cages.

Selling cages in pet shops

sheets of suitable material in all sorts of sizes. The best choice is white plasticized chipboard, as this is easy to work with and also easy to keep clean. Untreated chipboard has the disadvantage that the glue gives off toxic gases. This is not healthy for your birds. You can also use multiplex, which is also easy to work with, but it needs to be treated with a non-toxic environmentally friendly paint. It is a bit more difficult to keep clean and you need to repaint it once in a while. The advantage is that you can use another colour than white, which the birds find more relaxing.

The most common breeding cages are completely solid apart from the front wall, where a front panel is inserted. You can make this

The minimum measurements for breeding cages are 50 cm long, 40 cm high and 40 cm wide. Bigger is better, especially when the young are there. If the nesting box is attached to the outside of the cage then you can maximise the birds flying space.

The most commonly used floor covering in breeding cages is aviary sand. It is advisable to make a drawer for the sand which you can easily remove and clean. The easiest solution is a metal tray. If you make your cages yourself, you need to take into consideration that sand and bits of seeds will get between the drawer and the walls. If you make the cages so that the tray fits in perfectly, then you will have problems removing it if a lot of mess gets stuck in the gaps.

Flights

You can make as many flights of as large a size as you have space available. Once the young birds are independent you can place them in here. They then have more space available to develop further. You can also place breeding birds in flights during the resting season when they need to get into shape for the next breeding season or the exhibition season. If you want to keep hens and cocks separately in the resting season you need to have at least two flights.

Heating

Strictly speaking, heating is not actually necessary to get your birds through the winter. If they have a dry and sheltered night accommodation or if they are kept in a breeding room they can get by without heating. The cold is less of a problem to them than the dampness so typical to our winters. If you want to breed in the winter, which a lot of breeders do so that they have grown birds available for the showing season, then you should install heating. It doesn't have to reach tropical temperatures, as this is just a waste of electricity,

Red-browed Firetail

Zebra Finch, male
grey

10 to 15 °C is enough. You then don't have to put on your winter coat every time you're going to feed your birds. Another advantage is that those birds which have been to a show don't have to acclimatise when they come back. Otherwise show birds constantly move from a warm environment to a cold one and vice versa. Constant temperature changes increase the risk of illnesses.

If you do use heating make sure that the air doesn't become too dry in the aviary. Especially in the incubation period a humidity of 60 to 65% is necessary to let the eggs hatch normally. If the air is too dry, then the membrane around the embryo will harden and the chick will later not be able to free itself from the egg.

Lighting
Plenty of daylight is important, as your birds will slowly waste away in dark rooms and the breeding results will be disappointing. If you are going to build a breeding room, remember to integrate plenty of windows. It is best to place one or more transparent panels in the roof, as they will ensure plenty of light from above. You will usually have to rely on neon tubes to reach a sufficient amount of daylight. Time switches will make sure that the lighting is always switched on

and off at the same time. This ensures the regularity which is most like the lighting situation in the wild. If you have to switch the lights on and off manually variations will occur in the length of daylight which will throw the birds off balance. They will unexpectedly start moulting or abandon their nests, for example. It is best to let the light turn on and off at fixed times. The ideal amount of daylight is 12 to 15 hours in 24 hours. To make the changes from darkness to light less abrupt you should use automatic dimmers.

Oxygen
To keep your birds healthy you need to make sure that enough oxygen gets into their home. You can ensure this with the help of ventilation systems and cantilever windows. To keep vermin (mosquitoes) outdoors gauze blinds are usually installed. The gauze can become clogged up by dust, so you need to clean it regularly.

Behaviour
The behaviour of finches varies from species to species. Some are very social and live in colonies, some live in colonies during the resting period but separate from the group as pairs during brooding, whereas others live solitary lives.

Black-headed Munia

Some species are not aggressive but quite dominant, such as Zebra Finches. They will often be the first on the food bowl and also the first to choose a nesting box. Java Sparrows, Japanese nightingales and weaver species can sometimes disturb the brooding of other species and even steal the young and eggs. When choosing the species for your aviary take this into consideration if your aim is to breed finches.

When young birds are just about independent you can sometimes tame them. This will require a lot of time and patience every day. It is also important to observe the birds every day. You will get to know the hierarchy in the aviary and you can intervene in time if necessary.

It is obvious that this hobby requires some time. You don't only need time to look after your birds every day, but you also need to get to know your birds, which means that you need to spend approximately fifteen minutes a day observing and enjoying them. You will then know right away if a bird is not well or if something else is wrong. If you don't have this time then you have too many birds or too little time to look after them properly. You should then ask yourself whether it might be better for your birds if you stop this hobby.

Gouldian Finch

Breeding finches

Before you start breeding birds you need make sure that a number of prerequisites are fulfilled. The birds must be in good condition, fit to breed and at least a year old.

Breeding process

Experienced breeders usually slowly raise the number of light hours and the temperature to prepare the birds for the breeding season, especially when the breeder wants the birds to breed in winter. Use a time clock and a heater. This method resembles natural processes, as in the wild breeding starts when the days lengthen and the temperatures rise.

These are, however, not the only stimuli the birds react to. When spring comes, nature is full of new life. The trees and shrubs are green and insects reappear. This means a better menu. In winter, the natural resting period, birds only find little and very one-sided food. When this changes in spring

it puts the birds into brooding mood, even more than just the light and the temperature. Some bird species only start reproducing when they are sure that they will find enough food for their young. In the wild this is usually during or just after the rainy period. Although some breeders feed the same food all year round, the natural method (i.e. that the diet is adjusted to the seasonal offer) is preferable.

Make sure that your birds get enough gravel and calcium in the breeding period. Hens need it to lay good eggs. If you breed in breeding cages, you can separate the hens and cocks during the rest period and pair them up in the breeding cages later on. If you are going to breed birds in a

communal aviary and there are several birds of one species, then it is best to mark the birds with rings so that you can tell later which ones are the parents.

Make sure that the bird accommodation offers an excess of nesting boxes in different styles. Then there will be enough choice to prevent the birds from fighting. Also offer them plenty of nesting material, such as sisal ropes, coconut fibre, hay and moss. You can put the moss in the nests to start with, as it will keep the humidity level constant. You will not need to interfere with the nest building any further, as the birds can do it much better anyway and they also have a lot more time for it.

When the birds come into breeding mood they will start building their nest as soon as they get the opportunity. If they are in good breeding condition, you will find the first egg after a week. Finches usually lay four to six eggs. The incubation time can vary per species. Fertilised eggs usually hatch fourteen to twenty days after incubation started. You can recognise a fertilised egg by its colour. It will turn darker after a few days of incubation. You can also buy special test lamps. An unfertilised egg stays more or less transparent, whereas you can see blood vessels and the heart developing in fertilised eggs after

a few days.

You should offer your birds bath water more often during the breeding season. When the young have hatched they may bathe four times a week. You will also need to give your birds some extra food, such as egg food. You need to refresh this at least once a day. You may also want to add live food to your birds' diet, which you can also buy in handy deep-freeze packs. Not all bird species like live food, as it depends on what they eat in the wild. You may only feed germinated seed if it is absolutely free of mould.

Most species can be ringed five to eight days after they hatched. You can order rings from the different bird associations. The ring size varies from species to species. Have a look in bird magazines in which the ring sizes are given or ask the relevant person at your association. It is important to keep a good breeding logbook. In this you can note the batch, the ring numbers, when the young were born, if the parents are feeding them well and further information. You can then use these notes when selecting the birds with which you want to breed in the following season.

Most finches are independent after six weeks and they can then be separated from their parents. It is best to place them in a separate breeding or show cage for a week

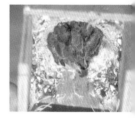

Different kinds of nesting opportunities

Possible problems during breeding
The brooding process doesn't always run as smoothly as described above. Try to keep an eye on your finches to find out what the causes may be. The most common problems are:

Unfertilised eggs
The birds you paired up don't really get along. If they cannot get used to each other you should separate them.
The birds are too young. Put them back into the aviary again and try again later, or break the pair up and give them older partners.
The mating wasn't successful due to loose perches.

Eggs are fertilised but don't hatch
The air is too dry in the aviary or sometimes the humidity is too high. A hygrometer will tell you the humidity in the birds' accommodation. The ideal humidity is between 55 and 65%.

Eggs are pricked and thus leak
The parents' nails are too long. Trim them.

Eggs have been laid but the hen doesn't want to incubate
You can place the eggs with a pair that broods well.
The cock is chasing the hen. Note such characteristics in the breeding logbook.

Young are not fed or only badly
Here, too, it might be an idea to transfer the chicks to another nest with young of approximately the same age. It is also common to transfer chicks to another nest if there are only one or two young. A nest of three to four young usually develops better as the chicks keep each other warm.

Young are attacked
The father is usually the culprit. Insert a partition in the breeding cage under which the chicks can hide.

Young Gouldian Finch

Photos on the next page:
Top: Bullfinches building a nest
Middle: nest young Black-throated Finches
Bottom: young Greenfinches

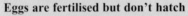

before releasing them into the aviary. They can then become independent in peace. Spray millet is quite a good food to help your birds become independent. When releasing the youngsters into an aviary it is best to put some older birds with them. They can function as teachers and show the babies where to find food and water. After the chicks have been taken away the parents will normally start laying the next batch of eggs straight away. Don't let the pairs breed all year long and limit the batches of eggs to two, three at the most. Give your birds a few months of rest after that. They will then not become exhausted, and you will still be able to enjoy your breeding birds the next year.

Young finches often have an adolescent plumage which differs widely from that of their parents. The chicks' plumage has a natural protective colour. The youngsters will normally moult at three months old and the adult plumage will then appear. The wing feathers often only moult in the second year.

Breeding logbook

A good breeding logbook is essential to trace the origins and the inheritance of your birds. What should you note? Here's an example with some standard information.

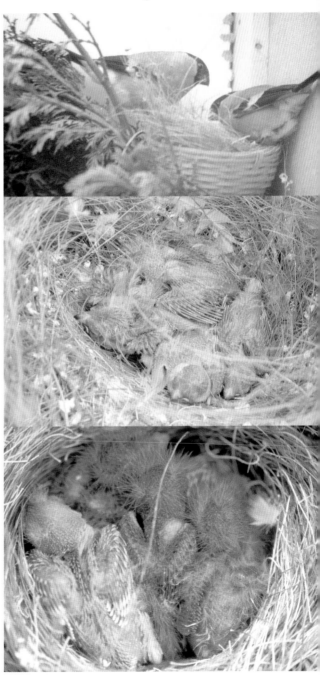

Greenfinch with
young

Young Bullfinches

Breeding logbook example

Breeding year: 20..
Cage number:
Species:

Data cock:
Ring no:
Colour:

Data hen
Ring no:
Colour:

1st batch
Date mating:
Date 1st egg:
Number eggs:

Number fertilised:
Date hatched:
Date ringed:
Date flown out:
Ring nos. young:
Colour young/ remarks:

2nd batch
Date mating:
Date 1st egg:
Number eggs:
Number fertilised:
Date hatched:
Date ringed:
Date flown out:
Ring nos. young
Colour young/ remarks:

Ringed bird

You can extend this form however you wish. The important thing is that you note down all the necessary information. You will get to know your birds better this way, and you can then give the buyers of your birds the right lineage. The way in which you keep your breeding logbook can be simple, from a few loose papers in a folder to a computer database. You can buy whole computer programmes for this purpose. You can transfer the details from the breeding cards to another register in which you note each bird's data, such as ring number, lineage, colour, show results, etc.

To be able to tell the birds apart you need to ring them. You can order bird rings from bird associations.

Shows

Hundreds of bird shows are held throughout the UK in the autumn. These are competitions in which the results of the breeding season are judged.

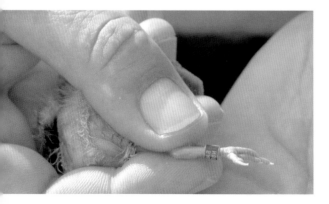

Useful contacts

Any local association will have a show at some point. The specialist clubs hold their shows on a regional level, but they also organise national shows. The best birds also go to the bigger regional shows and district competitions.

At the very top, there are also the world championships, which are held in a different European country each year, under the wing of the COM (Confederation Ornithologique Mondial). All species of birds are present at such a show: canaries, exotic birds, parrots, etc.

If you want to receive more information about associations, specialist clubs and shows, see Useful Contacts.

AUSTRALIAN FINCH SOCIETY (UK)
Foxhall Cottage, Foxhall, Kirkliston
West Lothian EH29 9ER

AVICULTURE SOCIETY OF THE UNITED KINGDOM
c/o Bristol Zoological Gardens
Clifton, Bristol BS8 3HA

BRITISH BIRD COUNCIL (UK)
1577 Bristol Rd. South, Longbridge, Birmingham B45 9UA

FOREIGN BIRD ASSOC. (UK)
96 Mitcham Lane
Steatham, London SW16 6NR

FOREIGN BIRD BREEDERS ASSOC. (UK)
Ray's Farm, Smelthouses, Summerbridge
Harrogate, North Yorks HG3 4DJ

FOREIGN BIRD ENTHUSIASTS CLUB (UK)
137 Dorchester Rd., Parkstone, Poole, Dorset

FOREIGN BIRD FEDERATION (UK)
4 Haven Crescent, Werrington, Stoke-on-Trent, Staffs ST9 0EY

FOREIGN BIRD LEAGUE (UK)
48 Twickenham Rd., Newton Abbot, South Devon TQ12 4QF

GOULDIAN FINCH SOCIETY (UK)
2 Dahlia Close, Burbage, Leicester LE10 2TB

INTERNATIONAL ORNITHOLOGICAL ASSOC. (UK)
62 Northwood Dr.
Sittingbourne, Kent ME10 4QS

NATIONAL COUNCIL FOR AVICULTURE (UK)
22 Foxearth Rd., Selsdon, Surrey CR2 8ED

SOCIETY FOR CONSERVATION IN AVICULTURE (UK)
87 Winn Rd., Lee, London SE12 9EY

WAXBILL FINCH SOCIETY (UK)
7 Walsingham Court, Chaddlewood Plympton, Plymouth, Devon PL7 3WN

ZEBRA FINCH SOCIETY (UK)
309 North Rd., Darlington, Co Durham DL1 2JR

Pin-tailed Whydah

Your birds' health

Birds are living creatures which can also become ill. Nursing a bird is not easy, especially not for a beginning enthusiast.

You can easily recognise an ill bird by its behaviour: it is less lively, sleeps a lot, raises its feathers, the eyes are dull or watering, and it has sometimes lost so much weight that you can see the sternum sticking out. If you think that your bird is ill, contact the vet as soon as possible. Try to explain the symptoms as clearly as possible. Look at the eyes, is the bird gasping for air, what do the faeces look like, how does it behave, is it eating well, is it sleeping well, is it sitting on its food bowl all day long? If necessary, the vet can examine the faeces and prescribe the appropriate medication. Make sure that your bird cannot catch a cold during the transport and cover the cage well.

Moulting
Birds change their plumage every year. The old worn-out feathers fall out and new ones replace them. This process normally occurs at the end of the summer and takes approximately six weeks. It is a natural process which every bird goes through. They will sometimes be less active, but this will improve once the moult is over. Moulting demands a lot of energy. If you make sure that your birds get enough egg food during the moult it will be over quickly and you will have beautiful birds at the end. After the moult, the birds are ready for the next show season.

Young birds moult within a few weeks after they have become independent. They change their adolescent plumage for their adult feathers. They will then get their full colour. The dull colours are replaced by the vivid, bright colours of the adult birds.

Prevention

Nursing birds is not easy and prevention is always better, so here are a number of tips.

Hazards in the house

• Make sure that other pets, such as dogs and cats, cannot get near your bird's cage. If you let your bird out of its cage, make sure that the cat is not in the same room and that all the doors are closed.

• In the kitchen your bird is at risk of burning itself on the stove. Don't let your bird fly in the kitchen or cover the stove.

• Birds can seriously harm themselves if they fly at the window at full speed. They don't expect a window to be there. In the most serious case, they can break their neck. In the first few days, only let your bird fly when it is dark. It will then get used to the size of the room and will not fly against the window as quickly in the daylight. There is a far smaller risk when you have drawn the blinds or curtains, of course.

Gouldian Finches, male and female

Star Finches

Page 33:
Gouldian Finches,
the male on the
right

• Birds can get stuck between doors that are being opened or closed. A bird walking on the floor is especially at risk. Be careful that you don't tread on your bird if it is walking on the ground.

• Remove poisonous houseplants or at least keep them out of the room where you let your birds fly. When buying new houseplants ask whether they are poisonous for pets.

General preventive measures
• Prevent excessive growth of nails and beaks by providing perches of suitable thickness

and plenty of gnawing opportunities (twigs, iodine blocks). If the nails need to be trimmed, use sharp nail scissors. Hold the nail against the light so that you can see where the blood vessels are. Make sure that you don't cut into them. If the foot does start bleeding try to stop it by holding it in cold water, but it is better to singe it closed with a burning cigarette, for example.

• Only feed your birds food which they are meant to have and never let them share your food. Fat, spiced foods and lots of sugar are harmful to their health.

Finches

- Don't let your birds catch a cold; make sure that they are not exposed to draughts.

- Prevent vermin in their cages. Use an insecticide before you prepare the cages for the breeding season. Birds can suffer from blood mites, especially young birds in the nest.

- Keep flies and midges out as far as possible by placing fly nets in front of open windows and doors. Mosquitoes can cause pocks in canaries.

- Also check for mice regularly. Try to keep the aviary as mice-free as possible. If you see traces of mice (such as droppings and evidence of gnawing) start fighting them as soon as possible. They turn into a plague faster than you can imagine. Mice cause unrest among birds at night and spread diseases, they soil the floor, smell and cause damage to the aviary.

- You can generally prevent a lot of diseases and suffering by paying good attention to hygiene. Make sure that cages, feed and drink bowls and perches are cleaned regularly. This prevents a lot of problems.

- It is best to contact the vet if you encounter broken wings or legs.

Species

There are many different species of finches which can be kept in an aviary very well. There is a bird to suit every taste.

Colour Canary
recessive white

Canaries

The canary is one of the most popular cage birds. It is a very popular pet bird because of its song.

Canaries are generally divided into three groups:
• Song canaries
• Colour canaries
• Type canaries

The song canary is obviously kept for its song. There are three species of song canaries, which are the Harzer, the Waterslager and the Timbrado. To a layman the songs of the different types might seem the same, but to a song breeder the songs of the colour canaries sound more like screams. Song canaries are specifically selected for their song quality and each species has its own song ('tour' in the breeders-jargon). Only the cocks sing.

Colour canaries are often kept as pet birds in the living room, but they are even more often kept as aviary birds. The canary is quite suitable for beginners, as it doesn't demand a lot in terms of care and breeds quite easily. Show breeders almost always breed them in breeding cages and often use one cock for several hens. You can also breed them in an aviary. This works best if you place twice as many hens in the aviary as cocks.

You can buy special nesting bowls (Harzer bowls) in pet shops, but a nesting box made of bars is also suitable for canaries. Sisal rope is good nesting material for canaries. A canary lays approximately four to six blue-green speckled eggs. When a canary has laid an egg, you remove it and replace it by an artificial egg. After the third egg has been laid you put the real egg back. Then all the eggs hatch at the same time. If you don't do that there might be three days age difference between the first born and the last born chick, because the hen starts brooding from the first egg. The last chicks often stay behind in the nest and also die quicker.

Young canaries are independent when the V-shape appears in the tail, which is approximately after six weeks. It can happen that the parents pluck the young. This usually happens after they have left the nest. The parents want to start with a new nest and use the chicks' feathers as nesting material. If this happens, you can put the young into a special baby cage which is hung onto the breeding cage. The parents cannot reach the chicks then, but they can still feed them through the bars. When there are young you should feed extra egg food. It is also advisable to feed extra germinated seeds and some green food.

Colour canaries are bred in almost all colours. Although most people think that canaries should be yellow, the original colour is green with black stripes. The red canary developed from crossing in the Black-hooded Red Siskin. Colour canaries are divided into several groups:
Pigmented, which are just as the wild form.
Lipochromes, here the pigment has disappeared and the yellow, red or white (secondary) colour remains.
Mosaics, i.e. birds with a standardised marking on the breast, wings and head.

The type canaries are specifically selected on the basis of format, model, posture and/or plumage. The following species are being bred:
Frilled species, here the plumage structure has changed. The feathers are often longer and often curl in various places.
Posture species. They need to hold themselves in a certain stance and stand tall on their legs.

Red intensve and red non-intensive

Agate yellow mosaic

Song Canary
Timbrado

Couple yellow mosaic
Agate red intensive
Agate red mosaic
Isabel red non-
intensive

Form species. They are bred specifically to fit into a certain form/model. They are often quite big around the chest area.
Crested species. They display a crest on their head.
Marked species. The most popular one of these is the lizard canary with its scaly marking and an unmarked head.

As you can see, there is enough choice if you want to start with canaries.

Advantages

• Canaries don't have special demands concerning caging and care.
• They breed very easily.
• The male has a beautiful song.
• There are lots of colours and types.
• There is plenty of choice.
• The purchase price of canaries is reasonable.
• They are not aggressive, even towards other species.
• Breeders and enthusiasts generally know a lot about these birds.
• They can cope quite well with the cold.

Disadvantages

• They will destroy any plants that you want to put in your aviary.
• You need to supplement the red canaries' food with red food colourings to keep them red.
• They are sensitive towards pocks (which are transferred by

mosquitoes) and they will almost always die of them. You can vaccinate them against this disease. The vaccine is often bought in bulk by the associations and all the birds are then vaccinated at the same time.

European songbirds

Our local birds, which are called European songbirds, have become very popular as aviary birds. They may only be kept as aviary birds if certain prerequisites are fulfilled. In the past, only seven species were allowed to be kept as aviary birds. Now that the laws have changed, all songbirds may be kept in captivity, but only after they have been fitted out with a solid ring issued by a recognised bird association. This ring must display a letter code which is different per species. The letters correspond with a certain standard. You need to be able to prove the origins of the parent birds. In the past, European songbirds were often used to breed hybrids with canaries. Although this is still being done, breeding genetically pure birds has increased in recent years. This is partly thanks to clubs specialising in these birds, where breeders can exchange their experiences.

The European songbird is not usually kept as a pet bird, but you can quite often find a shed or a house with a cage housing a song thrush or chaffinch. The cocks of both species are kept because of their beautiful song. There are even song contests for chaffinches. Here the tunes per minute are counted and the bird with the most tunes is the champion. You can get special singing cages for these competitions.

If you want to breed European songbirds, it is best to keep them in pairs in separate breeding cages. If you keep several pairs of one species together they will often start fighting in the breeding season. In the wild most species also have their own territories during the breeding season.

You can, however, keep different species together, although the best breeding results are still achieved in cages where only one pair is kept. You can also get good breeding results if you keep one pair in an aviary with other species; you can even keep and breed them together with some parakeet species.

You can buy special goldfinch seeds in pet shops, which you can use as food for chaffinches and also for most other European species. Besides the seeds, you also need to offer fresh egg food and live food every day during the breeding season. You can also buy animal food in deep-freeze

packs (mealworms, buffalo worms, pinkies). Fresh weed seeds (which you can pick yourself) are also very popular. You can also buy special weed seed mixes in pet shops.

European songbirds are very sensitive to intestinal disorders; coccidiosis is most common. This disease is caused by a parasite that attaches itself to the intestinal wall. In serious cases this disease is fatal. You can recognise coccidiosis by swollen intestines which often turn blue and by the bird's hunched position. The faeces become very watery (diarrhoea). Young birds which are just becoming independent and are moulting are particularly vulnerable to this disease. You can prevent and/or cure this disease by giving appropriate medication. It is best to treat breeding birds for a month before the breeding season and to give preventive antibiotics twice a week when the chicks have been separated from the parents. As soon as the young birds have their full plumage you can stop feeding antibiotics. You can get antibiotics from your vet. Always read the instructions on the package first!

It is impossible to deal with all the European songbird species in this book and we have thus made a selection.

Redpol

Greenfinch, pastel agate

Bullfinch

There is hardly any difference between cocks and hens in the case of the goldfinch. The male has a slightly bigger mask, but if subspecies are crossed with each other this difference can vanish. The cock almost always has a golden-yellow glow on its chest. You can see this particularly well if you hold the bird in your hand and blow its chest plumage to the side. The most obvious difference is the wing bend, as this is completely black in grown males and a sort of faded brown in adult females. It is more greyish in young birds in their adolescent plumage.

When a goldfinch is in breeding mood its beak will become almost totally white; the cock will also start 'dancing' by turning its tail and body. Goldfinches usually breed in the tops of trees and shrubs two to three metres high. The brooding season is from the end of April to August and the birds often breed two and sometimes even three times in one season. Goldfinches prefer white nesting material; this is usually white sheep's wool in the wild. The nest is made of some hair and feathers. Some sisal rope and non-greasy cotton padding will do in the aviary. The eggs are light pink with some speckles. Young goldfinches haven't got their parents' beautiful colour yet as this only comes through after the adolescent moulting. They would

Goldfinch

The goldfinch (*Carduelis carduelis*) is very popular due to its exotic plumage. It is very common in Europe and you will find them everywhere, in the countryside as well as in cities, in parks, graveyards and in gardens. The goldfinch has a lot of subspecies and those that live with us in the summer go to southern Europe or northern Africa for the winter. The species that stay here in the winter are the bigger species that breed in Scandinavia. You can thus see goldfinches all year round, but they are not all the same.

otherwise be easy prey for enemies when they fly out. Different mutations have occurred among goldfinches and even some mutation combinations, such as brown, agate, pastel, satinet, white-headed, opaline, pied (white-throated), Isabel and aganet.

Greenfinch

The greenfinch (*Carduelis chloris chloris*) is, as its name indicates, mainly green. It often breeds in Europe and you will find it anywhere. You will find them rummaging around on rose hips in the autumn in particular. You can see a clear difference between male and female greenfinches. The hen is only green on the tail and mostly brown otherwise with markings on the back. The cock doesn't have these markings and it also is a lighter green with a yellow spot under the throat, where the hen is white.

The greenfinch also breeds high up in trees and shrubs. The nesting material consists of grass stems. You can replace these by coconut fibres in the aviary. The nest is sometimes finished off with some feathers. The eggs are light pink to bluish with some speckles. Different mutations have occurred in greenfinches, including brown, agate, satinet, pastel, pied and Isabel, which is a combination of brown with agate.

Chinese Greenfinch

Bullfinch

You can easily recognise the bullfinch (*Pyrrhula pyrrhula europea*) by its flat head and its short arched beak. The upper beak has a small hook which makes it easier for the bird to peel seeds. The cock is vividly coloured with a red chest and belly, whereas the hen is more greyish-brown in colour.

Bullfinch male

Siskin male

Breeding Siskin,
female on the nest

The nesting material consists of coconut fibre. The hen lays five to seven bluish eggs. The following mutations and colours have appeared in bullfinches: brown, pastel, diluted, yellow and topaz.

Siskin

The siskin (*Carduelis spinus spinus*) is the only spinus species in Europe. The other real siskins only appear in Central and South America. In winter you can see hundreds of them descend on football fields, graveyards, plantations and alder thickets and, in true acrobatic style, pick the seeds out of the alder cones. They are thus often called alder siskins.

European bullfinches differ from the closely related Asian species by two red feather tips on the middle of the back. The Asian bullfinches don't have these. There are two European species: the smaller one which can be found in western and southern Europe and the bigger one which lives in northern Europe. Bullfinches are very peaceful birds by nature, which you can also approach quite closely in the wild. In an aviary they will often come and eat from your hand after a while. This tameness and the vivid colours have made them very popular with bird breeders.

The nest needs to be spacious and protected by some green twigs so that the hen can brood in peace. It is advisable to give the cock the opportunity to sit in front of the nest so that he can feed the hen.

Although no subspecies are mentioned in the literature, there are some differences: there are cocks with or without chin spot. The eyebrow stripe also differs; on siskins with chin spots it starts near the eye, on siskins without chin spots it starts at the beak. You can also see differences among hens: there are some which are more or less white on the chest and those that are a sort of yellowish.

There is a clear difference between male and female siskins. The male has a black cap and sometimes a chin spot and he is a green-yellow colour. The hen is lighter in colour and almost white on the front with black markings. Siskins are, like bullfinches, very calm birds and when leaving the aviary you have to make sure that there isn't one sitting on you somewhere. It would definitely not be the first time a bird escaped this way!

Siskins brood both half way up and at the top of the aviary. Here, too, you need to camouflage the nest with some greens. The nesting material consists of coconut fibres, sisal rope and feathers. The following mutations/ colour variations are known in siskins: brown, agate, pastel, dilute, phaeo, satinet, ivory (blue) and Isabel. These colours are also often combined with each other.

Siskins can be fed on seed mixes. The mixes available in pet shops contain extra black seed which they love.

Redpoll

The redpoll (*Acanthis flammea cabaret*) belongs to the same family as the linnet and the twite. It has a number of subspecies, which, apart from the small one (*cabaret*), includes the larger species, the white-tailed, the Icelandic and the Greenlandic redpoll. As far as the type and behaviour are concerned they are very similar to the siskin, and in winter you can often see them gathered in alders and birches. The redpoll can easily be identified by its red cap and it also lacks the yellow of the siskin.

Redpol

When they turn two, cocks get a red chest colour, whereas on hens the chest remains grey-white with black striping. They brood in northern Europe, and in summer the days are even longer there than they are in western Europe. To breed siskins it is advisable to give them at least fifteen hours light a day. As far as behaviour, care and illnesses are concerned the redpoll is very similar to the siskin and the goldfinch. The following mutations and colour variations are known among redpolls: brown, agate, Isabel, opaline, phaeo and dark factors.

Advantages of European songbirds

• There are many species in all sorts of colours and sizes.
• They are winter-hardy.
• They can easily be kept in a communal aviary, except the crow-like species.

Bullfinch, male

- Almost all species can be bred.
- Many species are excellent singers.

Disadvantages of European songbirds
- Most species are susceptible to coccidiosis and need to be treated regularly.
- They need to have special rings.
- It is often problematic to keep several pairs of one species together during the breeding season (it is no problem outside the breeding season).

Waxbills

Zebra Finches
The zebra finch *(Taeniopygia guttata)* is probably the most popular aviary bird of them all. It belongs in the waxbill category. Almost anyone who keeps birds or ever kept birds has had these chirpy Australian birds in his aviary at some point. More than a hundred colour variations have been bred from zebra finches. The original colour is grey and this wild colour is still very popular.

In the wild this bird lives a nomadic life and moves through all of Australia. You can always find it near watering places. They live in large groups and brood in colonies. Their food in the wild consists of all sorts of grass seeds and some insects. As aviary birds, they thrive on a basic mix of tropical seeds and some egg food, grit and some green food once in a while. In the wild zebra finches breed shortly after the rainy period, as this is when there is the largest supply of fresh grass seeds. As aviary birds they also like high humidity. You can ensure this by offering them bathing water several times a week, which they will definitely love.

Breeders who breed zebra finches for shows almost always do this in breeding cages of at least 40 x 40 x 40 cm. They also breed well if you have several pairs in an aviary together. They will definitely start incubating then. Zebra finches are quite brutal and dominant towards other birds. If a zebra finch feels like it, it might even occupy the nest of another bird, even if there are already eggs in there. They will also be the first on the feed bowl to pick out the tastiest seeds. This makes them less attractive for some

Zebra Finches
blackface grey

breeders and it is a reason why many switch over to other birds.

Zebra finches are not picky concerning their nesting box and their nesting material. They'll take anything they can get. It is easy to see the difference between the sexes: the males have an orange-brown spot on the cheek, black chest markings, chestnut flanks and the beak is also a little redder. The hens miss these markings.

Advantages
- This bird doesn't have many demands.
- Breeds easily.
- Low purchase price.
- Strong health.
- Not particularly sensitive to the cold.
- If they are used to it, they can live in a communal aviary with other species.
- Lively birds which are available in all sorts of different colours.

Disadvantages
- They are quite brutal and dominant, but not really aggressive.

Society Finch
Society Finches *(Lonchura domestica)* don't exist in the wild. They have been created in Japan as hybrids of different types of Manias. Society Finches have often been used as foster parents · for different species of waxbills. I

once saw five different species of chicks in the nest of Society Finches, all of which were raised without any problems. Luckily, there has been a trend towards letting waxbills brood naturally, but if there hadn't been Society Finches before there certainly wouldn't be as many waxbills for sale, or only at very high prices.

In the sixties, the usually pied Society Finches were selected towards single-coloured birds, partly by hybridisation with Black-headed Munias. This means that these birds have become worthy of being shown. There are also different types of mutations, besides the original mocha-brown there are also red-brown, grey, pastel, faded-wing, ino, crested

Society Finch, available in several colours

Society Finch

have the same measurements as those for zebra finches. They also eat the same food as zebra finches.

Advantages
- Ideal birds to brood eggs of other birds in the case of brooding problems.
- They are cheap to buy.
- They are available in different colours.
- They have no special demands concerning their care.

Disadvantages
- The appearance won't tell you whether it is a hen or a cock, the song will tell you.
- Breeding in aviaries with other pairs is difficult, you therefore need a lot of space for breeding cages.

and frilled. From the pieds, birds have been selected according to their colour patterns. Some specialist breeding clubs have made the Society Finch popular as an exhibition bird. You can find the contact details of clubs in the Useful contacts.

Society Finches breed easily. They prefer half-open nesting boxes. You can offer them grass or coconut fibre as nesting material and some sisal rope to finish off the nest. They can be kept together with other species without too many problems. Breeding might be difficult in an aviary, however, as they will all try to get into one nesting box to sleep. They are easily pushed aside by other birds in the aviary. This is why they are usually bred in breeding cages, which should

Gouldian Finch
If you see a Gouldian Finch *(Erythrura gouldiae)* for the first time you will think it was painted. This vividly coloured bird with all its distinctive colours is a real gem in any aviary. The Gouldian Finch originates in northern Australia. There are three species in the wild: the black-head, the red-head and the less common orange-head, which is often called yellow-head. The Gouldian Finch is heavily protected in the wild; the whole population is estimated to be no more than 1,500 birds in the wild. A number of breeding

programmes have been started to ensure the survival of these birds in the wild.

Luckily there is larger supply of Gouldian Finches as aviary birds and they are being bred all over the world. In the sixties, after the export ban from Australia, they were too popular with dealers and natural selection for quality was out of the focus. All the eggs were put under Society Finches and the Gouldian Finch even forgot how to brood. Even today, Gouldian Finches have the reputation of being very weak birds which need to be kept at a minimum temperature of 30 °C during the day and at 5 °C at night!

If you intend to keep these birds in an outdoor aviary, you should buy your birds from a breeder where they were already kept outdoors. It is best to buy them in the summer or in early autumn so that they can easily adapt to the colder nights. In the winter they need access to a frost-free shelter at night.

It is very easy to tell cocks and hens apart. The hen has duller colours but the same markings as the cock. Gouldian Finches can easily be kept in a communal aviary, even with several other pairs. Make sure that there are always excess nesting boxes. A special nesting box has been developed for Gouldian Finches

Gouldian Finch couple

Gouldian Finches
above: female
below: male
Blue mutations

Yellow red-headed
Gouldian Finch

which you can buy in pet shops. It is a closed nesting box with a round entrance hole and a small landing on the front where the cock often sits to hold watch. These birds always mate in the nesting box, which means that it has to be more spacious than nesting boxes for other species. They will also start brooding in a slightly larger breeding cage.

Gouldian Finches have a strong preference for dark nesting material (hay, coconut fibre). In the wild they usually brood in splits or holes of trees. It is darker in these spots, so the chicks cannot be spotted as easily. Nature has found a solution here: Gouldian Finches are born with luminous papillae around the beak, so the parents know exactly where to put the food. When these papillae dry up after the young have left the nest, they are independent. When the Gouldian Finch becomes fertile, the male's beak colour becomes almost white with a red or yellow spot and the hen's beak becomes almost completely lead-grey.

Young Gouldian Finches have not yet got their parents' bright colours, as they would then be easy prey for their natural enemies. Young birds are very sensitive to changes in their environment. After you have separated them from their parents you should place them in a flight from which they shouldn't really be moved

again. The move to another cage can even cause the chicks to stop moulting and to remain in half their adolescent coat for a full year, even if the new cage is exactly the same as the old.

These birds should be fed on a good exotic mix supplemented with Japanese millet (which they love), millet spray, egg food, grit and some minerals. If you want to let your birds bring up their chicks themselves, then you also need to add some pinkies and buffalo worms to their daily menu, as these contain vital proteins. Some mutations have occurred in Gouldian Finches, such as the white-chested, pastel, dilute, yellow, blue and cinnamon (brown).

Gouldian Finches are very sensitive to airway mites. These mites live in the birds' throats and stomachs and they irritate the birds very badly. Birds often sneeze when they are infected. If you don't do anything about it, it will get worse very quickly. Your birds can even die of it. The mite can be passed on to other birds too. You can easily treat your birds against airway mites by putting one or two drops against ear mites into their neck. It will usually offer relief within a day. Keep on observing your birds closely, as the mites' eggs can hatch after a week and everything may start again.

Advantages

- They are very colourful birds, which are pleasant to look at.
- Hens and cocks can easily be told apart.
- They can be kept together with other birds and even with several pairs.
- They don't need a special diet.

Disadvantages

- Young birds cannot be moved without them becoming stressed.
- They are very sensitive towards mite infections.
- They are sometimes a little too quiet: they can easily sit on a perch completely still, even if they are totally healthy.
- Wrong selection often leads to weak birds being offered for sale. Be very careful therefore where you buy your birds. Tip: ask the breeder about care and caging, as this will help you to prevent some problems.

Shafttail

The Shafttail *(Poephila acuticauda)* originates from Northern Australia. There are two different species, i.e. the red-beaked and the yellow-beaked. Orange-beaked birds occur in the transitional region, and it is not a separate species but a transitional form. You can easily recognise the Shafttail by its tail feathers, which are very long in comparison to its close relative, the Black-throated Finch

(Poephila cincta). The Black-throated Finch has a black bib and the same breech-markings, but it also has a black beak and no long tail feathers. The Masked Finch has only a small bib and a mask around its beak. The beak is yellow and the length of the tail feathers is between that of the Shafttail and that of the Black-throated Finch.

It is very difficult to see a difference between the male and the female Shafttail. In the case of the cock, the colour on the head is a light grey and the bib and breech-marking is a little bigger; in the case of the red-beaked species, the beak is also often a deeper red. As far as feeding and care are concerned, the Shafttail has similar demands as the Gouldian Finch, although it is not necessary to feed extra Japanese millet.

Brown Black-throated Finch

Shafttails

Shafttail

Diamond Firetail

Shafttails can be kept well both in communal aviaries and in breeding cages. They can be quite dominant, although they are not normally too aggressive towards other birds. However, there might be problems in the breeding season if you keep several Shafttails together, or if you keep them together with Black-throated Finches. If they don't fight for their own territory there is a big chance that the young are hybrids between these two species. Shafttails breed both in closed and in semi-open nesting boxes. Hay, coconut fibre and sisal rope are all accepted as nesting material. The following mutations are known in Shafttails: brown, Isabel, ino, grey and pastel.

Advantages
• They are beautiful, active aviary birds.
• The birds are generally healthy.
• They are easy to breed.
• They have a pleasant call.
• They are not too expensive to buy.
• They don't need any special care.

Disadvantages
• It is difficult to tell the sexes apart, you can often find the transitional orange-beaked form.
• They are quite aggressive towards others of their kind, especially in the breeding period; they can be kept together without too many problems in the resting period (after the breeding period).

Diamond Firetail
The Diamond Firetail *(Stagonopleura guttata)* originates in South-Eastern Australia and is a more sturdily built bird. Its call is also easy to recognise. There is hardly any difference between the cock and the hen, but the hen is a little more lead-grey on the head. Diamond Firetails need to have plenty of flying space, as they become fat very quickly.

They can be kept in a brooding cage but the measurements need to be bigger than those for other waxbills. The minimum size is 80 x 40 x 40 cm. It is better if they are kept in flights, simply because they become fat very quickly. In a communal aviary the Diamond Firetail can be very dominant

towards other birds of a similar or smaller build. They can, however, quite easily be kept with other European species and neophemas (a parakeet-species), for example. The care and breeding are similar to those of the Shafttail. The following mutations are known of the Diamond Firetail: yellow-beaked, brown, Isabel, dilute and opaline.

Advantages
- Very active birds with a distinctive call.
- They are very strong and can easily cope with the cold.
- They don't need any special care.
- They are not particularly expensive as far as purchase is concerned.

Disadvantages
- It is difficult to see a difference between hen and cock.
- They become fat very quickly.
- They are very dominant in an aviary.

Star Finch
The Star Finch *(Neochmia ruficauda)* originates in Western, Northern and Eastern Australia. The nominate form has an almost white belly and the sub-species *(N. clarescens)*, which is kept by breeders, has a yellow belly. It is easy to tell hens and cocks apart. The male's red mask is a lot bigger and the yellow on its belly is also a lot more intensive.

These birds can easily be kept in communal aviaries, and they can also be kept outdoors in winter as long as they have access to a frost-free night shelter. They also breed easily in breeding cages. Care and breeding are similar to those of the Shafttail. When the hen is ready for brooding she often gets a black stripe on her beak. The following mutations are known of the Star Finch: yellow-beaked, pastel and pied.

Advantages
- Beautiful colourful birds.
- There are obvious differences between the sexes.
- These birds can easily be kept with other birds and with several pairs.

Star Finch

Diamond Firetail

Star Finch

- They are reasonably priced.
- They don't need any special care.

Disadvantages
- They need frost-free shelter in the winter.

Red-headed Parrot Finch
Parrot Finches *(Erythrura psittacea)* are primarily green birds, often with red and blue markings. The different species are found in a wide distribution area, from Malaysia to New Guinea and Australia. There are ten different species with a number of sub-species, of which the red-headed and the tricoloured Parrot Finches (Erythura trichroa) are the best known. They are very lively birds which are always active. In an aviary with plants they will be less obvious because of their green plumage, but you will still get to see them a lot because they are active flyers. There is hardly any difference between hen and cock, the male has a slightly deeper red on the head and often has a few red feathers in the anal region.

Red-headed Parrot Finch

Red-headed Parrot Finches are very suitable for communal aviaries, but they need to have a frost-free shelter available in the winter. They breed in all sorts of nesting boxes or even build their own nest in shrubs or behind conifer twigs and they make a sort of tunnel as an entrance. The nesting material in the aviary consists of grass and coconut fibre. The following mutations have developed: sea-green, pied, yellow black-eyed and lutino.

The care is almost identical to that of the Shafttails. They love bathing and they should have clean bathing water available every day.

Advantages
- They are lively aviary birds.
- They don't need any special care.
- They can easily be kept in the aviary with other species.

Disadvantages
- It is difficult to tell the sexes apart.
- Because these birds are so active the tail is often damaged on the mesh, especially in smaller spaces.
- They need a lot of flying space.

Java Sparrow
The Java Sparrow or Java Finch *(Padda oryzivora)* was one of the first waxbills to be imported at the end of the eighteenth century. They originate in South-Eastern Asia, where they can be a real pest for the farmers by raiding rice fields. They have been bred a lot as songbirds and have become

Finches

popular show birds through their always tight plumage. They can be bred both in an aviary and in breeding cages. They can also be kept together with several pairs.

You need to keep a close eye on these birds. It is quite common to have a more aggressive individual in the aviary, which raids the nests of the other birds. It can sometimes go well for a few years until you suddenly have a trouble-maker in your aviary. They usually brood in closed nesting boxes and the nesting material consists of grass or hay and coconut fibre. Java Sparrows lay up to six to nine eggs which hatch 21 days after the first egg has been laid, as long as they have been fertilised.

It is difficult to tell the sexes apart, but the cocks have a slightly bigger beak. The underside of the V-form of the beak is sharper on cocks. On hens the underside is rounder. The eye-ring is also of a deeper red in the case of the cock, especially in the breeding period.

Besides the wild colour, the white Java Sparrow is also very popular. This white form has been selected from the pied. To keep the format and the plumage of the white variety at a high standard, they are usually crossed pied x white and vice versa. These crossings also bring forth pied chicks, which you

can distinguish from the white chicks straight after birth. The pied ones have a black spot on the beak whereas the white birds have a white beak. The following mutations have occurred in Java Sparrows: besides the pied and the white birds, there are also isabels, pastels and opalines.

Java Sparrow

Java Sparrows are winter-hardy, which means that they can be kept outdoors all year round as long as they have been outdoors from the summer. The feeding consists of a tropical or budgerigar seed mix, which should be complemented by paddy (unpeeled rice), egg food, grit, germinated seeds and some green food. Java Sparrows love to bathe, which is why you should regularly offer them fresh bathing water.

Five-coloured Munia

White-headed Munia

Advantages
- They always have a nice tight plumage.
- They are robust birds.
- They don't need any special care.
- They breed very easily.
- They are very lively birds.

Disadvantages
- There is hardly any difference between the sexes.
- They can be quite aggressive towards other species.

White-headed Munia

Munias belong to the large genus of lonchuras, to which Munias, Yellow-rumped Mannikin and Society Finches also belong. The White-headed Munia *(Lonchura maja)* exists in Southern Thailand, Malaysia, Sumatra, Java and Bali. There is hardly any visible difference between cocks and hens. Birds with a whiter head are often cocks, the hens are often darker in colour. This is not always the case, however. The colour of the head varies depends on the region where the birds come from.

When you buy White-headed Munias in a shop it is best to buy a number of them and to give them all differently coloured foot rings. You can then keep a close eye on which birds form pairs with each other. If you buy your birds from a breeder who knows his birds, he can tell you the differences between cocks and hens and you will be sure that you are really buying a pair.

As far as care is concerned, they have the same demands as the Shafttails and their behaviour and breeding is the same as that of the Java Sparrow. Munias often suffer from long nails, which you thus need to check regularly. Cut the nails to just before the quick, which you can see if you hold the nail to the light.

The advantages and disadvantages of the White-headed Munia are the same as those of the Java Sparrow.

You can find more information about White-headed Munias and other lonchuras in our description of the Society Finch.

Dusky Munia

The Dusky Munia (*Lonchura fuscans*), which can only be found on Borneo, is the least contrasting Munia. The colour is almost completely black-brown with a very vague scale-like marking. There is no visible difference between hens and cocks, the only difference is the cock's song. They are quiet birds, which can be kept and bred in both breeding cages and aviaries. They can also be kept together with other species. It is advisable, however, not to keep them together with other lonchuras, as this could lead to unwanted hybrids.

They need to have access to frost-free shelter in the winter. Their care is similar to that of the Shafttails. You can use both semi-open and closed nesting boxes. Their favourite nesting material is grass or hay and coconut fibre.

Advantages
• They are quiet birds.
• They can be kept in a communal aviary.

Dusky Munia

• They don't need any special care.

Disadvantages
• There is no visible difference between the sexes.
• Their colour is plain, if you can see this as a disadvantage.

Melba Finch

The Melba Finch *(Pytilla melba melba)* lives in Angola, Katanga and Northern Rhodesia. The genus *Pytilla* also includes the Aurora Finch, the Red-winged red-faced Pytilia, the Red-faced Pytilia, the Red-winged Pytilia and the Orange-winged Pytilia.

Outside the breeding season they can be kept together with other small finch-species, but they are often very aggressive in the breeding season, especially towards others of the same species. It is best to keep them in pairs during the breeding season,

Melba Finch

buffalo worms. Live food also should be fed outside the breeding season. In an aviary with plants they will go searching for lice, flies and spiders. They will also happily accept germinated seeds. Also make sure that you offer them regular bathing opportunities.

Both parents brood on the three to five eggs, which hatch after thirteen days. The young stay in the nest for three weeks and are then partly fed by their parents for another few weeks. In the first few days the young are primarily fed with live food. After approximately a week they are also fed seeds. Make sure that you offer the birds very fine seeds during that time, such as White French Millet and different weed seeds. An ino mutation is known of the Melba Finch.

Melba Finches couple

and sometimes you even have to separate the cock from the hen!

They are best kept in an aviary with plants, where they build freestanding nests in conifers or shrubs. A semi-open nesting box is also often used, in which they build a sloppy nest made of grass stems, finished off with feathers. They can be kept in an outdoor aviary in the summer, but in the winter they need to be kept in a heated night shelter with a minimum temperature of 10 °C.

The feeding consists of a good tropical mix enriched with grass and weed seeds, millet spray, a general seed mix and live food, such as mealworms, pinkies and

Advantages
• Vividly coloured birds, especially the cock.
• Very lively in an aviary.
• There are clear differences between the cock and the hen. The hen lacks the red and ochre on head and chest.

Disadvantages
• Very aggressive in the breeding season.
• Their diet needs some attention.
• They need to be kept in a heated environment in the winter.
• Not exactly cheap to buy.

Gold-breasted Waxbill

The Gold-breasted waxbill *(Amandava subflava)* can be found in an area from Senegal to Ethiopia and Kenya, the sub-species *A. s. clarkei*, which is also called Yellow-breasted waxbill, lives in an area from Zaire to Tanzania and South Africa. The Gold-breasted waxbill is one of the smallest seed-eating birds in the world: it only measures nine to ten centimetres!

There is a clear difference between cocks and hens. The hen lacks the red around the eye, and the chest and belly are a lot duller in colour. They can easily be kept with other species or with others of their own kind, both outside and during the breeding time. You can even achieve good breeding results by keeping them in more spacious breeding cages. They need to be kept in frost-free spaces during the winter. They brood both in all sorts of nesting boxes and in some plants in the aviary. The nest is made of grass stalks and coconut fibre; the entrance is made as a tunnel. To check the four to six white eggs, you carefully need to take them out of the nest with a spoon. The same applies to the young when they need to be ringed.

Feeding and care are the same as for the Melba Finch.

Advantages

- They can easily be kept with other species and with others of their own kind.
- There is an easily visible difference between the sexes.
- They are beautifully coloured and marked.
- The purchase price is reasonable.

Disadvantages

- The small size makes them difficult to catch and also makes checks on the nest difficult.
- Their care needs special attention.
- They need to be kept frost-free in the winter months.

Gold-breasted Waxbill, male with young

Gold-breasted Waxbill, male

Red-cheeked
Cordonblue

Red-cheeked Cordonbleu

The Red-cheeked Cordonbleu *(Uraeginthus bengalus)* exists in large parts of Central Africa. The nominate form is found in Senegal, Eritrea, Western Kenya and Uganda. The hen lacks the red spot on the cheek and its blue is also less strong. There are five subspecies to the *Uraeginthus* genus: the Red-cheeked Cordonbleu, the Blue-breasted Cordonbleu, the Blue-capped Cordonbleu, the Common Grenadier and the Purple Grenadier. The whole genus of *Ureaginthus* has a strikingly long tail in comparison to other waxbills.

Red-cheeked Cordonbleus are best kept in an aviary with plants, they will quickly feel at home here and start brooding. They need to have access to a frost-free space in the winter months. These birds will brood in self-made

nests in shrubs or trees, but they will also happily use nesting boxes. The nesting material consists of grass stalks, coconut fibre and sisal rope. The hen covers the nest on the inside with her feathers.

A batch consists of three to six white eggs, which hatch after twelve days. Both cock and hen are involved with the brooding. The hen generally incubates the eggs at night. The young are completely independent after five weeks and the parents usually lay another batch of eggs then. Especially if they have young, the birds need to have live food. There are also some mutations of the Red-cheeked Cordonbleu, which are the yellow-cheeked and the brown. Red-cheeked Cordonbleus can also be easily kept in communal aviaries and they are very agile.

The care is similar to that of the Melba Finch.

Advantages
- Beautiful colourful birds ideal for aviaries.
- There is a clear difference between the sexes.
- They can easily be kept together with other species.

Disadvantages
- Their care needs extra attention, especially in the breeding period.

• They need to have access to frost-free accommodation in the winter.

Green Singer

The Green Singer *(Serinus mozambicus)* is one of the best known African finch species. Its great song in particular has made it very popular. The Green Singer has eleven sub-species which live all over Africa. The Green Singer belongs to the Cinis, just as the canary.

Hen and cock can easily be distinguished, as the hen has a marking on the chest which looks like a necklace, and it is a little duller in colour. In some of the subspecies the hen is completely yellow on the chest. You can breed Green Singers both in breeding cages and in aviaries. You need to be aware, however, that they can be very aggressive towards other aviary inhabitants, especially if they belong to smaller species, such as the White-rumped Seedeater and other species of the same colour.

If you want to breed Green Singers in a communal aviary, then it is best to keep them together with slightly bigger species, as these can defend themselves better. The most popular nesting boxes are the semi-open box and the grid nesting box. Grass stalks and coconut fibre are used as nesting material and the nest is finished off with sisal rope and feathers. Young Green Singers look like the hen. Green Singers are also often used to breed hybrids with canaries. Especially the cocks from these crossings can sing very well. There seems to be a blue mutation of the Green Singer, but very little is known about this.

Green Singers

Their food consists of a good tropical mix supplemented with canary seeds, weed seeds and egg food. Grit must also not be missing. In the breeding period the diet should be supplemented with germinated seeds, green food and some live food. Although they can cope well with the cold, it is better to keep them in a frost-free environment in the winter.

Advantages

The cocks are great singers. There is a clear difference between the sexes.
• They can easily cope with the cold.
• They are beautifully coloured birds.
• Their care is not special.
• They can get very old (20 years and more)

Disadvantages
• They can be very aggressive in the breeding season.

Whydahs

Whydahs are divided into two groups: the real whydahs and the whydahs that belong to the weaverbirds. The real whydahs are brooding parasites, just as the cuckoo. The hens lay their eggs in the nests of other species (host birds) which then raise the young. Every whydah species has its own host bird. In the case of the Eastern Paradise Whydahs the host birds are the pytilia species, such as the Melba Finch, the Aurora Finch and the Orange-winged Pytilia. The young of the whydahs are similar to the young of the host birds in terms of colour, markings and sound and the parents therefore don't notice the difference. Besides the Eastern Paradise Whydah, the Pintail Whydah is also often kept as an aviary bird. This uses the St. Helena Waxbill as host bird. The whydahs belong to the genus *Vidua*.

You will only sporadically achieve breeding successes with these birds. Some breeding results are known of. You need to keep a whydah cock in an aviary with at least three hens and the right host bird. The host birds also don't always breed easily. If you get them all into breeding condition at the same time and keep them in a quiet, sheltered aviary, then you have a chance of success, although it will always remain a challenge. As far as food is concerned, they have the same needs as their host birds.

Whydahs are ornaments for your aviary, especially when the cock is in his nuptial gear. In the resting period, however, the cock has a simple plumage which is similar to that of the hen. It also loses its long tail feathers then. In the resting period its size is approximately thirteen centimetres, in the nuptial gear it is 35 to 45 cm! It is best to buy them when the cock's tail still has

Pin-tailed Whydah

to reach its full length. Otherwise the other birds in the aviary will become very unsettled when a bird with such a long tail is suddenly flying around in the aviary. If they can slowly get used to it they won't be afraid anymore. There are also other species of whydahs, but you will hardly ever find them in shops. Whydahs exist south of the Sahara desert. If you only want them in your aviary for ornamental reasons, then buying a single cock will be sufficient.

There are also whydahs which are closely related to the weavers, for example the Yellow-mantled Whydah. These species belong to the genus Euplectes. They have a shorter tail and brood as pairs in their own nests. You can see their relationship to the weavers at the head and from the shape of the beak. In contrast to weavers, the whydahs build their nests in high grass. To breed them in an aviary, you will need to make sure that they have access to high grass. Here, too, breeding success is the exception. The feeding is basically the same as that of the other whydahs.

Whydahs can interrupt the brooding of other birds, and you need to be aware of this when buying these birds. In the winter months they need to have a minimum temperature of 10 ᵒC. Their care is the same as that of the waxbills.

Advantages
- The cocks are ornamental for your aviary.
- They can be kept in communal aviaries without too many problems.
- They are not particularly expensive to buy.

Disadvantages
- They are very difficult to breed, you need to keep them together with host birds.
- They need to be kept warm in winter.
- The cock loses its beautiful colours in the resting period.
- Whydahs can disrupt the brooding of other birds.

Pin-tailed Whydahs
right: male,
left: female

Red Bishop

Orange Bishop

North-western Red-
billed Quelea,
couple

Weavers

Weavers owe their name to the way they build their nests. Whilst hanging from twigs and canes they weave sometimes enormous hanging nests. There are more than 270 weaver species, most of which live in Africa and Asia. Most weaver species are colony birds and they live in groups of sometimes thousands of birds. Weavers are also polygamous, which means that a cock often has several hens, sometimes up to six.

Just as in the case of the whydahs, most weaver cocks have a nuptial plumage and a resting plumage. In the resting plumage there is hardly any difference between cock and hen. They are very popular aviary birds because they weave interesting nests on twigs and mesh and because of their beautiful colours. The most commonly kept species belong to the following groups: Black Bishop (orange, grenadier, flames, black-bellied), the Village Weaver (small, large, egg-yellow) and the Red-billed Quelea.

Weavers are strong birds which can be kept in an outdoor aviary all year round. They can become very old. There are weavers which have lived in their aviary for a good fifteen years and whose age was not known when they were bought. Unfortunately they also have a bad habit: they like to raid the nests of other aviary inhabitants to use the nesting material themselves. It is thus advisable to keep them with bigger species if you want to breed. You need to be aware, however, that breeding successes with weavers are exceptions, but maybe this is exactly the challenge you are looking for? If you have an aviary and you don't necessarily want to breed, then weavers definitely shouldn't be missing.

As far as care is concerned, they don't have any special requirements. They'll eat almost anything you offer them. As a basic food you can feed them a tropical mix, canary seed, weed seeds, egg food, germinated seeds, green food and some mealworms.

Advantages
- They are usually vividly coloured birds with a lot of contrast in their plumage (cock).
- They are hardy and can cope well with the cold.
- They can get very old.

Finches

- They don't need any special care.
- Most species are reasonably priced.

Disadvantages
- They can be dominant and aggressive towards other aviary inhabitants.
- The breeding results are minimal.
- In a lot of species, the cock cannot be distinguished from the hen in its resting plumage.

Cuba Finch

Cuba finches *(Tiaris canora)* aren't only found on Cuba, but also in the whole of Central America and also in the northern regions of South America. There are five species of Cuba finches with several subspecies. The Cuba finch is the best known, followed by the Yellow-faced Grassquit *(Tiaris olivacea)* and the black-chested Cuba Finch *(Tiaris bicolor)*. The cocks are more noticeable in terms of colours and markings, the hens have very light markings and duller colours.

You can achieve good breeding results with Cuba finches, both in breeding cages and in an aviary. They look best in an aviary. Cuba finches can easily be kept in a communal aviary, although they will enter the nests of other aviary inhabitants once in a while! It is inadvisable to keep several (species of) Cuba finches in the same space during the breeding season, as the cocks will chase each other until there are casualties. They can be kept together in the resting period. Especially when birds have only recently been placed together, you need to keep an eye on them to make sure that peace is ensured.

The nesting material consists of grass stalks and coconut fibre. They prefer shrubs and small trees as nesting locations where they can build the nests themselves. If this is not possible a semi-open nesting box will also do. They make an entrance hole at the side of the nest. The three to four eggs are light green/ bluish and have red stripes. Both parents sit on the eggs. Incubation takes approximately twelve to fourteen days and the young leave the nest after approximately four weeks. The parents will often start with a new batch straight away. It is then advisable to remove the young from the aviary when they are approximately six weeks old, as there is a chance that the cock will chase the young because he sees them as rivals.

The care is similar to that of the Shafttails. Especially during the breeding period it is advisable to enrich the general food with some live food. In the winter it is best to keep them frost-free at a temperature of at least 10 °C. Cuba finches are reasonable singers.

Small Cubafinch male

Orange-breasted
Bunting: right male,
left female

This male has a
stronger red on his
belly due to a special
diet.

Advantages
• They are very distinctly marked
  birds.
• They can easily be kept in an
  aviary with other birds.
• They don't need any special
  care.
• It is easy to keep the sexes apart.
• They are fairly good singers.
• They are fairly easy to breed.

Disadvantages
• In the breeding season they are
  aggressive towards others of
  their kind.
• They need to be kept frost-free.
• They are quite expensive to buy.

American Finches
The group of American finches has
never become as popular as the
finch species of Africa, Asia,
Australia and Europe, despite the
beautiful colours of the cocks. But
why? Imported birds are regularly

offered for sale. The purchase price
varies a lot from very cheap to very
expensive. Breeding successes are
achieved regularly. The problem is
that it is often quite difficult to get
hens, and the hens of the different
species also look very much alike.
American finches exist in South,
Central and North America. The
best known species are: the Indigo
Bunting *(Passerina cyanea)* which
is deep blue, the Varied Bunting
(Passerina versicolor), the Painted
Bunting *(Passerina ciris)*, the
Orange-breasted Bunting
(Passerina leclancherii) and the
Lazuli Bunting *(Passerina
amoena)*.
Other American seed-eaters are:
the Blue-black Grassquit *(Volatinia
jacarina)*, the Ultra-marine
Grosbeak, which belongs to the
genus *Cyanocompsa* and has six
subspecies. The cock is primarily
cobalt to violet-blue and the hen is
almost completely brown.

As far as their food is concerned
they don't have too many
demands: a mix of tropical or
canary seeds enriched with weed
seeds (fresh, although semi-ripe is
better), grit, egg food, germinated
seeds and green food. It is vital to
offer them live food such as
buffalo worms and pinkies in the
breeding season. It is also
important to feed them weed
seeds. These contain a lot of
carotene, which they need to keep
a beautiful colour. Some finches
have nuptial and resting plumage,

just as weavers. In its resting plumage the cock looks just like the hen. It is obvious that you should offer your birds fresh drinking and bathing water on a daily basis.

American finches can easily be kept in a communal aviary, although they can be quite dominant in the breeding season, especially the Ultra-marine Grosbeak. If you want to breed it is best to keep them in pairs, just as European songbirds. The species from South and Central America should be kept at a minimum temperature of 10 °C in the winter months. Although the Painted Bunting would obviously prefer to be outdoors day and night all year round, as the North American species are winter-hardy.
Their song is beautiful, although some species hardly ever sing. The Ultra-marine Grosbeak will only sing when its young are leaving the nest and the Painted Bunting only sings in the middle of the night.

Advantages
- The cocks have beautiful colours.
- They can be kept in a communal aviary.
- They don't need any special care.
- Some species are winter-hardy.
- There is a clear difference between the sexes.

Red Cardinal couple

Disadvantages
- It is often difficult to get hold of hens of the right species.
- They can be a nuisance to other birds during the breeding season.
- Some species need to have heated winter accommodation.
- The colours fade if the birds are fed one-sidedly or if there are no plants in the aviary.
- You hardly ever hear them sing.

Cardinals
There are twelve different species of cardinals, most of which live in South American, although they can also be found in Central and North America. Although one of its names, 'Pigmy Cardinal' would have you believe that it belongs to the Cardinal family, the Black-crested Finch *(Lophospingus*

Red Cardinal

Red Cardinal couple

pusillus) belongs to a different genus. This genus is also noticeably smaller than the real cardinals, which are approximately the size of blackbirds. Some species have a crest whereas others have a smooth head.

The best-known species is the Yellow Cardinal (*Gubernatrix cristata*), which is primarily green in colour with yellow on the head, a black bib and crest. The hen has only very little yellow on the head and is more whitish in colour. The Northern Cardinal *(Cardinalis cardinalis)* lives in North America and the body of the cock is completely red including the crest and it has a red mask around the beak. The hen is yellow-brown in colour and the mask is quite vague, but the beak is bright red. The Red-crested Cardinal *(Paroaria coronata)* is very distinct with its red head, crest and chest, its white lower body and its grey back and mantle. There is hardly any difference between the sexes in this species. The hen is often a little smaller and its red is also less vivid.

Cardinals can easily be kept in a communal aviary with other birds of a similar size, such as weavers, thrushes and starling species. They can disturb the rest of smaller bird species, especially during the breeding period. They are best kept in an aviary with plants, and they also breed best here. They build

their nest in shrubs, conifers or in nesting baskets. As nesting material, they use twigs, grass stems, coconut fibre and hair.

Their feeding consists of a coarse seed mix (the ones for lovebirds or neophemas are ideal) enriched with paddy, oats, millet spray, safflower seeds, egg food and grit. During the breeding period they need to be given extra egg food, germinated seeds, green food, general food and live food, such as mealworms, maggots and ant eggs. They also need fresh drinking and bathing water on a regular basis. Cardinals are winter-hardy but it is better to offer them a night shelter where they can seek protection.

Advantages
- It is a robust, winter-hardy bird species.
- They don't need any special care.
- In some species there is a clear difference between the sexes.
- They can be kept together with species of similar size.
- They are easy to breed.

Disadvantages
- They cannot be kept together with smaller species.
- In some species there is only very little difference between the sexes.
- They aren't always easy to get; sometimes you see hardly any in shops and then you will suddenly find several species on offer again.